RETURN FROM EXTINCTION

THE MOUNTAIN GORILLA

LEONARD CLASKY

Gareth Stevens PUBLISHING

Please visit our website, www.garethstevens.com. For a free color catalog of all our high-quality books, call toll free 1-800-542-2595 or fax 1-877-542-2596.

Library of Congress Cataloging-in-Publication Data

Names: Clasky, Leonard, author.
Title: The mountain gorilla / Leonard Clasky.
Description: New York : Gareth Stevens Publishing, [2023] | Series: Return from extinction | Includes index.
Identifiers: LCCN 2022002030 (print) | LCCN 2022002031 (ebook) | ISBN 9781538280416 (library binding) | ISBN 9781538280393 (paperback) | ISBN 9781538280409 (set) | ISBN 9781538280423 (ebook)
Subjects: LCSH: Mountain gorilla–Conservation–Juvenile literature. | Rare mammals–Juvenile literature.
Classification: LCC QL737.P94 C527 2023 (print) | LCC QL737.P94 (ebook) | DDC 599.884–dc23/eng/20220119
LC record available at https://lccn.loc.gov/2022002030
LC ebook record available at https://lccn.loc.gov/2022002031Please visit our website, www.garethstevens.com. For a free color catalog of all our high-quality books, call toll free 1-800-542-2595 or fax 1-877-542-2596.

Published in 2023 by
Gareth Stevens Publishing
29 East 21st Street
New York, NY 10010

Designer: Olivia Lo Sardo
Editor: Caitie McAneney

Photo credits: Cover FionaAverst/Shutterstock; p5 Onyx9/Shutterstock; p7, 17 AndrewJBell/Shutterstock; p9 MaryAnnMcDonald/Shutterstock; p10 IslaVicek/Shutterstock; p11, 27 GUDKOVAudrey/Shutterstock; p13 TonyCampbell/Shutterstock; p14-15 BrinaLBunt/Shutterstock; p18 Denys.Kutsevalov/Shuttertstock; p19 Hanohik/Shutterstock; p21 Bemysolution/Shutterstock; p23 LiamWhite/Shutterstock; p24-25 KarenFoleyPhotography/Shutterstock; p29 KikiDohmeier/Shutterstock

Printed in the United States of America

CPSIA compliance information: Batch #CSGS23: For further information contact Gareth Stevens, New York, New York at 1-800-542-2595.

CONTENTS

Words in the glossary appear in **bold** type the first time they are used in the text.

MAGNIFICENT MOUNTAIN GORILLAS

You may never see a mountain gorilla in real life. That's because these wonderful creatures are found high in the mountains of Africa. Mountain gorillas are large, strong animals with calm natures. These massive **mammals** live together in groups called troops with **complex** social structures. In these groups, which are like families, every gorilla has a role, or part, to play.

Today's mountain gorillas are truly a marvel. Scientists predicted, or expected, that they wouldn't survive into the 21st century. Though their populations are small, these gorillas are still found in their native habitat, or natural homes. They are endangered, however, and **conservation** efforts are necessary for their survival.

CONSERVING ENDANGERED SPECIES

CONSERVATION EFFORTS HELP PRESERVE THE NATURAL WORLD, WILDLIFE, AND IMPORTANT RESOURCES. THE INTERNATIONAL UNION FOR CONSERVATION OF NATURE (IUCN) RED LIST OF **THREATENED** SPECIES WAS FOUNDED IN 1964. A SPECIES IS A KIND OF ANIMAL. THIS LIST SHOWS SPECIES' RISK OF GOING EXTINCT, OR DYING OUT. MOUNTAIN GORILLAS ARE LISTED AS ENDANGERED, OR AT A VERY HIGH RISK OF GOING EXTINCT.

Mountain gorillas live in a cloud forest, which is a forest dense, or thick, with trees and often covered in mist or fog.

THE PRIMATE CONNECTION

You might look at gorillas and think that they look and act a lot like humans. That's because humans and gorillas belong to the same group of mammals, called primates. Primates have hands, handlike feet, flat nails, and eyes that face forward. Monkeys, apes, tarsiers, and lemurs are part of this group. Gorillas share a common **ancestor** with all of these animals.

Like humans, gorillas are very intelligent. They can even learn some sign language! They carry their babies much like a human parent would. They live in groups just like we live in households. Scientists found that mountain gorillas like to play around in water like humans too.

THE EASTERN GORILLA

THE LARGEST LIVING PRIMATE IS THE EASTERN GORILLA. MOUNTAIN GORILLAS ARE A SUBSPECIES OF THE EASTERN GORILLA. EASTERN LOWLAND GORILLAS, MORE COMMONLY CALLED GRAUER'S GORILLAS, ARE THE OTHER SUBSPECIES. "SUBSPECIES" MEANS THEY'RE VERY CLOSELY RELATED, BUT SCIENTISTS PUT MOUNTAIN GORILLAS INTO THEIR OWN GROUP. MOUNTAIN GORILLAS WERE DISCOVERED AS A SUBSPECIES IN 1902.

Humans share around 96 percent of their **DNA** with gorillas.

MEET THE MOUNTAIN GORILLA

Mountain gorillas can be identified by their long, black fur. Adult males have a patch of silver hair on their back, which is why they're sometimes called silverbacks. Males can be up to 6 feet (1.8 m) tall and weigh up to about 480 pounds (218 kg). Females are a bit smaller. They can grow to 5 feet (1.5 m) tall and weigh around 215 pounds (97.5 kg).

Mountain gorillas are herbivores, which means they eat plants. They eat stems of vines, shrubs, herbs, bamboo, and fruit. They also eat roots and tree bark. The thick forests of Africa provide plenty of food for mountain gorillas.

MOUNTAIN GORILLA RANGE

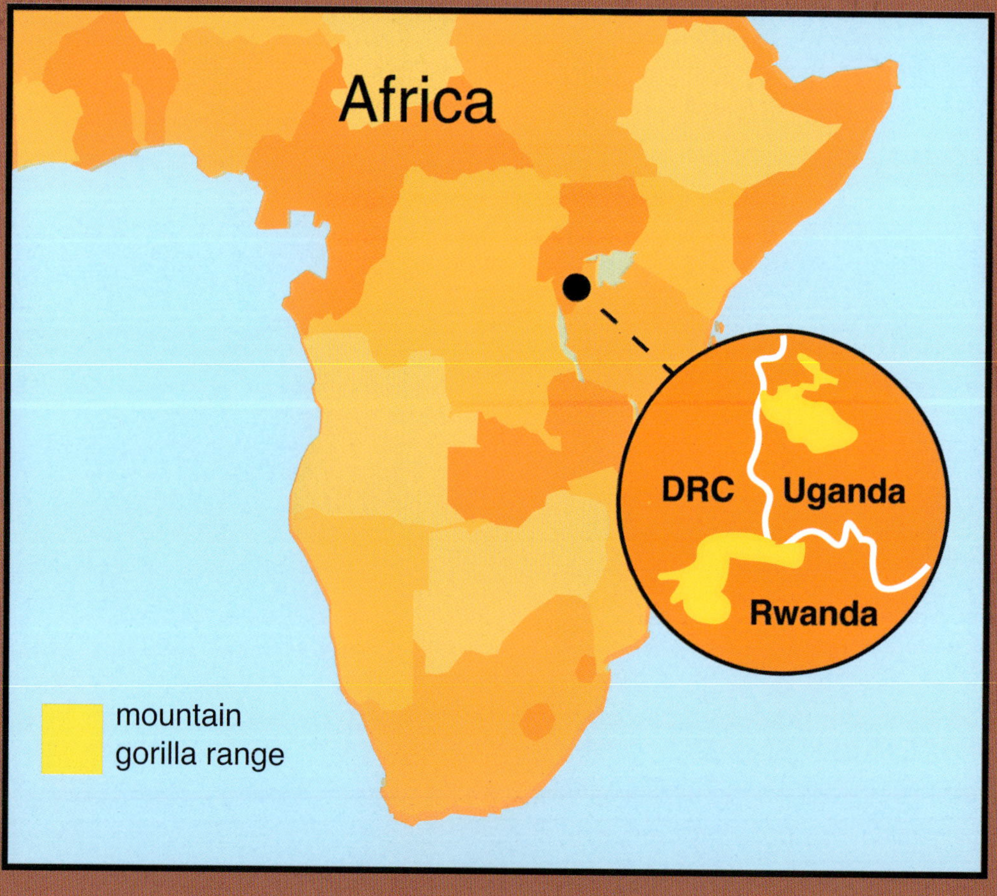

An adult male gorilla can eat up to 40 pounds (18 kg) of plants per day. While they can climb trees, mountain gorillas often nest in plants and leaves on the ground.

AT HOME IN THE MOUNTAINS

MOUNTAIN GORILLAS LIVE HIGH IN THE VIRUNGA MOUNTAINS, BETWEEN 7,200 TO 14,100 FEET (2,194.6 TO 4,297.7 M) ABOVE SEA LEVEL. THEY HAVE A SMALL RANGE IN THE DENSE CLOUD FOREST. THE AREA BELONGS TO THREE AFRICAN COUNTRIES: THE DEMOCRATIC REPUBLIC OF THE CONGO (DRC), RWANDA, AND UGANDA.

GORILLA FAMILIES

Scientists have discovered a complex social order to mountain gorilla troops. The silverback is the most **dominant** gorilla in the troop. It's often referred to as the "alpha male." Its job is to lead and protect the troop. When the alpha male feels challenged or threatened, it may pound its chest, roar, or throw things. The alpha male's main goal is to protect his troop, sometimes fighting to the death to ensure its safety.

Troops often have three to four adult females and a few younger males. Young and baby gorillas also make up families. Some troops include more than 20 gorillas!

GORILLA TALK

GORILLAS COMMUNICATE IN SEVERAL DIFFERENT WAYS. THEY VOCALIZE, OR MAKE DIFFERENT KINDS OF SOUNDS WITH THEIR MOUTH. THEY CAN BE REALLY LOUD! SCIENTISTS HAVE FOUND AROUND 25 VOCALIZATIONS, AND EACH MEANS SOMETHING SPECIFIC. FOR EXAMPLE, GORILLAS BURP LOUDLY WHILE RESTING, MAKE A HIGH CRYING SOUND CALLED WHINING WHILE EATING, AND HOOT TO ALERT ONE ANOTHER.

Baby mountain gorillas whine and whimper, just like human babies.

GROWING GORILLAS

Mountain gorillas have a slow rate of reproduction, or having babies. That's one reason they are at risk of dying out. Female gorillas only give birth to one baby at a time. If too many gorillas die before more are born, their population goes down.

For such a large animal, mountain gorillas are born very small. Newborn gorillas only weigh about 4 pounds (1.8 kg)! After they're born, baby mountain gorillas cling to their mother's fur. Babies drink their mother's milk for more than four years. Female gorillas reach adulthood when they're about 10 years old, and males around 15 to 20. Wild gorillas live for about 35 to 40 years.

KIDS AT PLAY

JUVENILE, OR YOUNG, MOUNTAIN GORILLAS ACT A LOT LIKE KIDS! THEY PLAY, CLIMB TREES, SWING FROM BRANCHES, AND CHASE EACH OTHER. SCIENTISTS BELIEVE THAT THIS PLAY HELPS TO KEEP THEIR FAMILY BONDS STRONG. SOMETIMES A SILVERBACK OR FEMALE ADULT GORILLA WILL PLAY WITH THE JUVENILES TOO. THEY'RE KNOWN TO MAKE CHUCKLING, OR LAUGHING, SOUNDS AS THEY PLAY.

When they're around four months old, baby gorillas begin to ride on their mother's back. They do this until they're two or three years old.

LIVES IN DANGER

For decades, mountain gorillas have interested the humans who study them. Scientists learned that these creatures depend on their families and on their habitats. As nomads, mountain gorillas travel together within a range of 10 to 15 square miles (26 to 39 sq km). Every night, mountain gorillas make themselves new nests out of fresh leaves. This is how they've adapted to their **environment**.

Unfortunately, people have put mountain gorilla lives at risk by destroying their habitats and harming troops. Because of this, mountain gorillas were listed as critically endangered. That meant that they were at an extremely, or seriously, high risk of dying out.

A GOOD SIGN

IN 2008, MOUNTAIN GORILLAS WERE LISTED AS ENDANGERED INSTEAD OF CRITICALLY ENDANGERED. WHILE THEIR POPULATIONS WERE STILL VERY MUCH AT RISK, SCIENTISTS BELIEVED THAT THEIR POPULATIONS HAD IMPROVED. TODAY OVER 1,000 MOUNTAIN GORILLAS ARE IN THE WILD. THIS POPULATION IS HIGHER THAN IT ONCE WAS, WHICH IS WHY SOME PEOPLE SAY MOUNTAIN GORILLA NUMBERS ARE BOUNCING BACK.

No mountain gorillas are held in captivity, or under human care. The only mountain gorillas in the world are wild.

DEADLY DESTRUCTION

Mountain gorillas have suffered from human activity, mainly habitat loss, hunting, and war. Habitat loss is the loss of livable land due to changes in the environment. This means the land can no longer provide everything a creature needs to survive. The environment may not be a safe place to raise young. It may not have any food sources or clean water. When this happens, animals have fewer places to call home.

As the world's human population increases, people are moving onto the land that mountain gorillas once freely roamed. They've cleared mountain habitats for livestock, farming, and building homes. People also use trees in many ways, including for firewood.

THE GORILLAS OF BWINDI

TODAY, MOUNTAIN GORILLAS EXIST ONLY IN TWO LOCATIONS: THE VIRUNGA MOUNTAIN RANGE IN CENTRAL AFRICA AND THE BWINDI IMPENETRABLE NATIONAL PARK IN UGANDA. ABOUT HALF OF THE MOUNTAIN GORILLAS LIVE IN THE NATIONAL PARK. THEIR HABITAT IS PROTECTED WITHIN THIS DENSE FOREST. PEOPLE CAN GO ON TOURS THROUGH THE NATIONAL PARK TO SPOT MOUNTAIN GORILLAS IN THEIR NATURAL HABITAT.

This mountain gorilla lives in Bwindi Impenetrable National Park. The word "impenetrable" means that something is closed, protected, or unable to be passed through. People can go on tours to see gorillas in the park, though!

THE EFFECTS OF WAR

In 1994, as many as 800,000 people were killed in Rwanda as part of a civil war, or a war between two groups within a country. Around the same time, unrest in the Democratic Republic of the Congo turned deadly. People were forced to leave their homes, and thousands fled to the forests of the Virunga Mountains.

However, these wars didn't just affect people. **Refugees** set up camps in the forests and cut down trees near mountain gorillas' forest homes. This put major stress, or strain, on the environment. The mountain gorillas' habitat changed very quickly in a short period of time.

SPREADING SICKNESS

WHEN REFUGEES ARRIVED IN THE VIRUNGA MOUNTAINS, ILLNESSES SUCH AS THE MEASLES OR EVEN THE COMMON COLD BEGAN KILLING GORILLAS. HOWEVER, PARK RANGERS AND CONSERVATION GROUPS WORK TO HELP THE GORILLAS AND GIVE THEM MEDICINE. MOST IMPORTANTLY, THEY EDUCATE PEOPLE ABOUT PROTECTING GORILLAS.

Park rangers and activists taught people how important it is to protect mountain gorillas. Their efforts helped mountain gorillas survive years of war.

POACHING PRIMATES

Poaching means killing animals illegally. Poaching was a major threat to mountain gorillas in the past. Some primates are poached for the pet trade or for wild meat, called bushmeat. While mountain gorillas aren't usually targeted by poachers anymore, they can become caught in traps set for other species.

In 2007, seven mountain gorillas were killed in Virunga National Park. News of the killings shocked and outraged people around the world. The crimes may have been carried out by people who were angry that they couldn't cut down the forests where gorillas live. The killers were never caught.

THANKS TO PARK RANGERS

PARK RANGERS HAVE VERY IMPORTANT, AND DANGEROUS, JOBS. THEY HAVE TO PATROL, OR WATCH, AREAS WHERE MOUNTAIN GORILLAS ARE LIVING TO KEEP THEM SAFE. HOWEVER, RANGERS ARE SOMETIMES HARMED OR KILLED BY POACHERS OR **REBELS**. IN APRIL 2020, REBELS KILLED 13 RANGERS IN VIRUNGA NATIONAL PARK OF THE DEMOCRATIC REPUBLIC OF THE CONGO.

Sometimes, poachers capture and sell young mountain gorillas. To steal a baby gorilla, poachers will usually kill its mother.

DIAN FOSSEY'S MISSION

Conservationist Dian Fossey changed the course of the survival of the mountain gorilla species. Fossey was an American scientist who affected the way the world thought about mountain gorillas. Before Fossey observed them, many people thought that mountain gorillas were **aggressive** and harmful. Fossey set out to prove them wrong.

Fossey worked with mountain gorillas for nearly 20 years. She was patient and gentle as she watched the animals. She **mimicked** their calls and movements. She gained their trust and was able to study their lives and social order. She also worked to stop poaching. In 1985, she was found dead in her cabin, possibly killed by poachers.

SETTING UP CAMP

IN 1963, DIAN FOSSEY VISITED AFRICA FOR THE FIRST TIME. SHE MET THE FAMOUS SCIENTIST LOUIS LEAKEY AND SAW HER FIRST MOUNTAIN GORILLA. SHE RETURNED IN 1966 AND FOUNDED THE KARISOKE RESEARCH CENTER IN THE VIRUNGA MOUNTAINS IN 1967 TO OBSERVE MOUNTAIN GORILLAS. THE CENTER, WHICH IS STILL OPEN TODAY, STARTED WITH TWO SMALL TENTS IN THE WILDERNESS.

DIAN FOSSEY'S LIFE AND WORK

January 16, 1932: Dian Fossey is born in San Francisco, California.

1963: Fossey travels to Africa and meets scientist Louis Leakey.

1966: Fossey returns to Africa to stay and research mountain gorillas in the Virunga Mountains of Rwanda.

1967: Fossey founds the Karisoke Research Center, where she observes mountain gorillas.

1974: Fossey earns her doctorate degree in zoology, making her Dr. Dian Fossey.

1977: A gorilla Fossey befriended and named Digit is killed by poachers. She sets up a special fund for people to patrol the area and keep the gorillas safe.

1983: *Gorillas in the Mist* is published.

December 27, 1985: Fossey is found dead in her cabin.

Fossey's work lives on in her book *Gorillas in the Mist* and the Dian Fossey Gorilla Fund International, a conservation group that helps mountain gorillas.

PROTECTING THE MOUNTAIN GORILLA

In 1971, the Virunga mountain gorilla population was only 275. By around 1978, the population had dropped to as low as 254. Starting in the late 1970s, conservationists started educating people about the falling mountain gorilla populations. They taught locals, including law enforcement officials, why conservation is important.

Conservationists also worked directly with gorillas. They gave them medicine and care. They worked with the gorillas to get them used to seeing people. This was important because it made ecotourism possible. Ecotourism is when people visit natural environments, sometimes ones that are threatened. These visits can bring attention to the needs of mountain gorillas.

Tourists must keep a certain distance from mountain gorillas. That keeps them from spreading illnesses to the endangered animals.

RESPONSIBLE ECOTOURISM

RESPONSIBLE ECOTOURISTS MAKE SURE TO LEAVE THE ENVIRONMENT AND WILDLIFE AS THEY FOUND IT. THEY CAN'T LITTER OR HARM ANY PLANTS OR ANIMALS. PEOPLE MUST WEAR MASKS WHEN THEY ARE AROUND GORILLAS. THIS HELPS PREVENT THE SPREAD OF HARMFUL SICKNESSES. THIS BECAME ESPECIALLY IMPORTANT DURING THE COVID-19 PANDEMIC, OR WIDE OUTBREAK OF DISEASE.

SUCCESSES AND CHALLENGES

In 1982, mountain gorilla populations hit their lowest point at only 242. Since then, the mountain gorilla populations have steadily increased thanks to conservation efforts to more than 1,000 in 2019. Protecting this species is dependent on daily efforts from national park rangers and conservation organizations. Ecotourism has also helped communities economically, encouraging locals to protect gorillas too.

The comeback of the mountain gorilla is a great success story. It's the only wild ape whose population is increasing. They are still at risk though—especially as human populations continue to grow, more land is taken over, and nations remain at war. New challenges and threats are sure to appear over time, so protection may always be necessary.

NEW THREATS

MOUNTAIN GORILLAS ARE FACING MORE THREATS AS PEOPLE START TO USE THEIR LAND FOR PROFIT. IN 2018, THE DEMOCRATIC REPUBLIC OF THE CONGO GOVERNMENT CONSIDERED ALLOWING OIL EXPLORATION IN NATIONAL PARKS WHERE MOUNTAIN GORILLAS LIVE. PEOPLE HAVE ALSO HARVESTED CHARCOAL FROM VIRUNGA NATIONAL PARK ILLEGALLY, WHICH RUINS THE HABITAT.

Conservationists, lawmakers, and everyday people have worked hard to save these gentle giants, and their efforts have been successful.

HELPING MOUNTAIN GORILLAS

Many people spend their lives working for the survival of mountain gorillas. Rangers protect them every day, risking their own lives. But you might want to help them too! Several conservation groups work to protect mountain gorillas, such as the African Wildlife Foundation. Some even help more than one kind of animal. You can choose to donate, or give money, to these groups. They use donations to carry out their conservation efforts.

You can also raise awareness. People must learn to value animals' lives. Educate the people around you about endangered animals, including the mountain gorilla. If enough people care about mountain gorillas, conservation efforts will continue for years to come.

CLIMATE CHANGE

CLIMATE CHANGE IS AFFECTING WILDLIFE AROUND THE WORLD IN MANY WAYS. LUCKILY, MOUNTAIN GORILLAS CAN STAND MANY DIFFERENT TEMPERATURES AND EAT A WIDE DIET. HOWEVER, THEIR RANGE IS VERY SMALL WITH NO OPPORTUNITY FOR GROWTH. WHEN GORILLAS HAVE TO CLUSTER TOGETHER, AND HUMAN SETTLEMENTS EXPAND BECAUSE OF CLIMATE ISSUES, DISEASES CAN SPREAD AND HABITATS CAN BE LOST.

Mountain gorillas don't pose a risk to people. They'd happily eat plants and play with their families all day. We shouldn't pose a risk to them either.

GLOSSARY

aggressive: Showing a readiness to attack.

ancestor: An animal that lived before others in its family tree.

complex: Having many parts.

conservation: Efforts to care for the natural world.

DNA: Part of the body that carries genetic information, which gives the instructions for life.

dominant: The most powerful or strongest.

environment: The natural surroundings for a person, plant, or animal.

mammal: A warm-blooded animal that has a backbone and hair, breathes air, and feeds milk to its young.

mimic: To copy.

rebel: A person who is fighting against their government.

refugee: Someone who is seeking a safe place to live, especially during a time of war.

threatened: In danger.

FOR MORE INFORMATION

Books

Bullard, Lisa. *Saving Mountain Gorillas.* Lake Elmo, MN: Focus Readers, 2021.

Ganeri, Anita. *Endangered Animals.* London, UK: Wayland, 2019.

Rissman, Rebecca. *Kings of the Mountains.* North Mankato, MN: Capstone Press, 2018.

Websites

Endangered Animals
www.dkfindout.com/us/more-find-out/special-events/endangered-animals/
Explore more about other endangered animal species around the world, such as the orangutan and panda bear.

Gorilla
www.ducksters.com/animals/gorilla.php
Learn more about gorillas, including their habitat, diet, and behavior.

Mountain Gorilla
kids.nationalgeographic.com/animals/mammals/facts/mountain-gorilla
Discover fun facts about the mountain gorilla with National Geographic Kids.

Publisher's note to educators and parents: Our editors have carefully reviewed these websites to ensure that they are suitable for students. Many websites change frequently, however, and we cannot guarantee that a site's future contents will continue to meet our high standards of quality and educational value. Be advised that students should be closely supervised whenever they access the Internet.

INDEX